Baby
goes to
Market

Baby

This one is for Nancy ~ A.

For David, Eva and Fred with love ~ A.B.

This story takes place in a West African market.

Its market stalls and market sellers are inspired

by markets known and loved by Atinuke,

the Nigerian author, and Angela,

the illustrator, who grew up in West Africa.

First published 2017 by Walker Books Ltd, 87 Vauxhall Walk, London SE11 5HJ ✪ Text © 2017 Atinuke ✪ Illustrations © 2017 Angela Brooksbank
The right of Atinuke and Angela Brooksbank to be identified as author and illustrator respectively of this work has been asserted by them in
accordance with the Copyright, Designs and Patents Act 1988 ✪ This book has been typeset in Schinn ✪ Printed in China ✪ All rights reserved

goes to Market

Atinuke ✪ Angela Brooksbank

WALKER BOOKS
AND SUBSIDIARIES
LONDON · BOSTON · SYDNEY · AUCKLAND

Baby goes to market
with Mama.

Market is very crowded.
Baby is very curious.

Baby is so curious that
Mrs Ade the banana-seller
gives Baby six bananas.

Baby is so surprised.

Baby eats one banana ...

and puts five bananas
in the basket.

Mama does not notice.
She is busy
buying rice.

Market is very crowded.
Baby is very hot.

Baby is so hot that
Mr Femi the orange-seller
gives Baby five juicy
oranges.

Baby grins.

Baby sucks one
orange ...

and puts four oranges
in the basket.

Mama does not notice.
She is busy buying
homemade palm oil.

Market is very crowded.
Baby is very cheerful.

Baby is so cheerful that
Mr Momo the biscuit-seller
gives Baby four sugary
chin-chin biscuits.

Baby claps.

Baby eats one
chin-chin ...

and puts three chin-chin
in the basket.

Mama does not notice.
She is busy buying
chilli peppers.

Market is very crowded.
Baby is very funny.

Baby is so funny that
Mrs Kunle the
sweetcorn-seller
gives Baby
three roasted
sweetcorn.

Baby
beams.

Baby eats one
roasted sweetcorn ...

and puts two roasted sweetcorn in the basket.
Mama does not notice.
She is busy buying flip flops.

Market is very crowded.
Baby is very naughty.
Very naughty pulling
on ALL the clothes!

Baby is so sorry that
Mrs Dele the coconut-seller gives
Baby two pieces of coconut.

Baby licks his lips.

Baby eats
one piece of
coconut ...

and puts the other piece
in the basket.

Mama does not notice.
Her basket is
very heavy.

Very, very
heavy.

And Mama thinks her
sweet baby must be
hungry by now!

"TAXI!"
Mama shouts.
"We need to get home
quick and fast!"

Mama puts her basket down.

"What is this?" cries Mama.
"Five bananas! Four oranges!
Three chin-chin biscuits!
Two roasted sweetcorn!
One piece of coconut!

I did NOT buy
these!"

"No, you didn't!"

laughs Mrs Ade
the banana-seller

and Mr Femi
the orange-seller

and Mr Momo
the chin-chin-seller

and Mrs Kunle
the sweetcorn-seller

and Mrs Dele
the coconut-seller.

"We gave those things to Baby!"

Mama looks at Baby.

Baby laughs.

Mama laughs, too.

"What a good baby!" she says.
"You put all those things straight
into the basket!"

Mama rides the taxi.
Baby goes to sleep.
"Poor Baby!" says Mama.
"He's not had one
single thing
to eat!"